"It's not what you find,
it's what you find out...
Understanding history is what the
Expedition Whydah project is all about."

—Barry Clifford

Real Pirates

· 1717 ·

The Untold Story of The Whydah
from slave ship to pirate ship

Barry Clifford

• Illustrated by Gregory Manchess ▪ Artifact Photography by Kenneth Garrett •

NATIONAL
GEOGRAPHIC

Washington, D.C.

"I was not a treasure hunter, although I was obviously hunting for treasure. I was a history hunter, an undersea salvor with a driving interest in bringing a great historic period back to life in a responsible way that an ordinary person could appreciate as well as a historian."

Silver pieces of eight from the pirate ship Whydah

How I Learned About Pirates

When I was a boy growing up on Cape Cod, I spent a lot of time with my Uncle Bill. He had a shack by the sea, and I would listen to him tell tall tales as he mended his fishing gear.

My favorite story was about the pirate ship *Whydah*, and her captain, "Black Sam" Bellamy, who was sailing to Cape Cod in the spring of 1717 to visit his girlfriend, young Maria Hallett.

Sam's ship was filled with gold and silver and jewels—including a ruby the size of a hen's egg—and Black Sam hoped that he and his ladylove would live happily ever after on the stolen booty. Instead, he, his crew, and all of the treasure sank to the bottom of the sea.

Uncle Bill told me that Maria witnessed the wreck, and how grief-stricken she was when she learned that it was Sam's ship that went down. He said Maria thereafter became a witch, and her only friends were a magical one-eyed cat and an old gray goat.

Before long, I figured out that Uncle Bill was exaggerating a little, but from those days on, the pirate ship was never far from my mind. As I got older, I learned that some of his stories were true. And I also learned about diving and how to find and explore shipwrecks.

After two years of searching, my team and I found the *Whydah*, and we have been bringing up her treasures ever since. We've discovered that some stories about pirates are really true, but that their lives were often far different from what's usually found in books or in the movies.

Those are some of the things this book is about. It is also about following your dreams, never giving up, and how teamwork can make dreams come true.

Outfitting the Slave Ship *Whydah*

With Christopher Columbus's first voyage across the Atlantic the European conquest of America began. The new land was incredibly rich; not only with gold and silver, but also with crops such as sugarcane and tobacco.

Much labor was needed to gain these riches. For over four hundred years, millions of people were forced to work in the mines and fields of the New World.

Since new diseases from Europe, as well as simple cruelty, caused the deaths of many Native Americans, Europeans soon began sailing to Africa with goods to be traded for human beings. Captive Africans were then taken to America to be sold as slaves. Slave ships then sailed back to Europe with cargoes of New World produce. This was known as "the Triangular Trade."

The *Whydah Galley* was one ship involved in this terrible business. Named after an African port, she was built in London in 1715 as a fast type of ship known as a "galley." Slavers liked fast ships since fewer captives died during quick voyages. In addition to the sails on her three masts, she could be rowed with long oars if need be.

She was also armed with eighteen cannon in case pirates attacked.

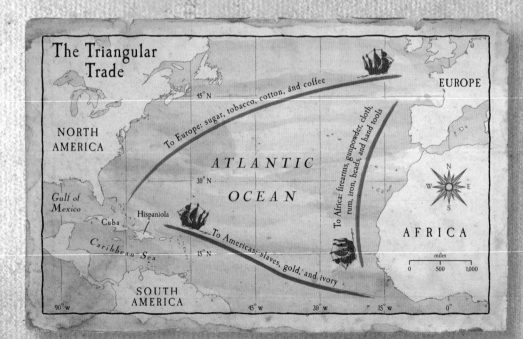

The Triangular Trade

NORTH AMERICA

Gulf of Mexico

Cuba

Hispaniola

Caribbean Sea

SOUTH AMERICA

ATLANTIC OCEAN

To Europe: sugar, tobacco, cotton, and coffee

To Americas: slaves, gold, and ivory

To Africa: firearms, gunpowder, cloth, rum, iron, beads, and hand tools

EUROPE

AFRICA

miles
0   500   1,000

45° N
30° N
15° N
90° w   45° w   30° w   15° w   0°

Trade was the life-blood of the New World.

Torn from their homes, captives were ferried out to waiting ships.

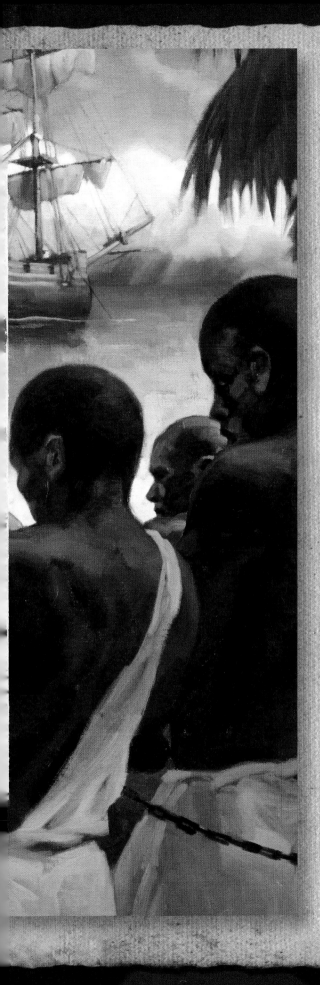

The Slave Trade

Slavery is one of humanity's most shameful crimes.

Added to the evil of unjustly depriving other people of their freedom, the trade in slaves taken from Africa was especially brutal and vicious.

When Lawrence Prince, captain of the *Whydah,* came to the coast of Africa, he traded his ship's cargo of such things as cloth, liquor, guns, and hand tools to local African nobles and merchants. Many of the people he bought in exchange were prisoners taken by other tribes in war.

They were loaded aboard the ship never to see their homes again. Many families were separated forever.

Conditions on board ship were frightful. In order to make money, the slavers crammed as many people aboard as possible. The *Whydah* could have carried as many as six hundred people below-decks in a space no bigger than one hundred feet long, thirty feet wide, and six feet high.

The captives would be allowed on deck twice a day, at most, for meals of boiled gruel and a drink of water. While topside, the slavers forced them to exercise. They spent the rest of the voyage crammed together in darkness. In such conditions, disease spread rapidly and many people died.

Once the *Whydah* reached port in the Caribbean, the captives were sold. They would spend the rest of their lives in a strange land as slaves in forced labor for other men.

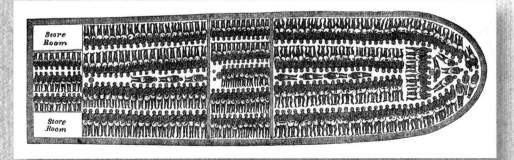

Diagram showing how captives were stowed aboard ship.

The Capture of a Pirate Prize

I think that Captain Prince was probably worried as he set sail for home with all of the treasure and rich cargo from the sale of the *Whydah*'s captives.

Thousands of pirates were swarming the Caribbean, robbing ships wherever they could. Captain Prince might have hoped that the *Whydah* would be too fast for any pirate who might spot her.

If so, he was wrong. Two pirate ships commanded by Sam Bellamy caught up to him in the Bahamas. Even though the *Whydah* was well-armed, Prince quickly surrendered.

This was not unusual. Pirate crews were larger and better-armed than those on slave ships. Since it made no sense to sink a ship one wanted to rob, pirates specialized in hand-to-hand combat. Sailors did not own any of the cargo and treasure being transported, and were not fighting men, and so had little reason to risk their lives resisting ferocious pirates.

Once Bellamy looked over this fine new prize ship, he took the *Whydah* over for his own. He gave Captain Prince his own vessel, and transferred his treasure, cannon, and other valuables to his new pirate flagship.

Bellamy had good reason to be pleased. According to court records, the *Whydah* treasure, by itself, was worth a fortune.

Pirates even used hand grenades!

Pirates often attacked by surprise at night.

Sam Bellamy & His Crew

I have spent so many years searching for the *Whydah*, and studying her history, that it seems as if I know some of her crew.

Sam Bellamy was originally from England. Old legends that I heard as a boy say that he came to Cape Cod as a sailor looking for a new start in life. Hearing stories of Spanish shipwrecks, he decided to find their sunken treasure, get rich, and marry his sweetheart.

Bellamy and his men didn't find any gold or silver. And so, they decided to turn pirate and rob ships instead.

Black Sam's crew soon grew to about 200 men. Most were British, but there were many other nationalities as

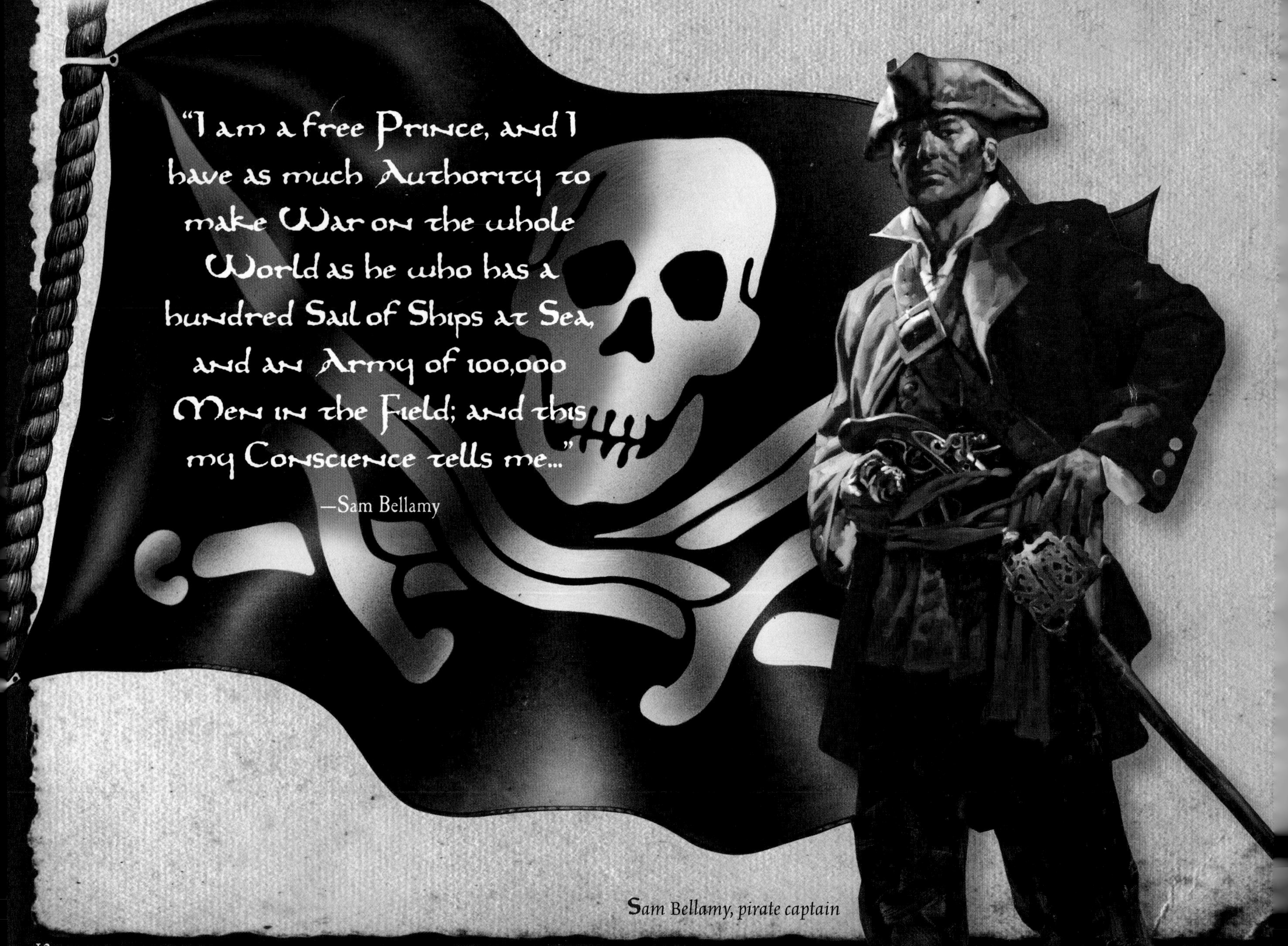

> "I am a free Prince, and I have as much Authority to make War on the whole World as he who has a hundred Sail of Ships at Sea, and an Army of 100,000 Men in the Field; and this my Conscience tells me..."
>
> —Sam Bellamy

Sam Bellamy, pirate captain

12

well—French, Dutch, Spanish, American colonists, three Native Americans, at least fifty Africans, and others. Most were former merchant sailors who were tired of hard work and low pay. Others were political and religious refugees. Many of the blacks were runaway slaves who were welcome to join the pirates.

Some of Bellamy's pirates did not even speak a common language. Even so, they worked together as equals.

One of the pirates was John King, who was sailing with his mother when they were captured by Bellamy. John decided that he wanted to become a pirate and talked them into letting him join. When

John's mother tried to convince him that this was a bad idea, he threw a tantrum and even threatened her.

Judging from what happened later, I think he should have listened. From his leg bone, scientists tell us John King was no older than eleven when he died.

Hendrick Quintor, a black man from Amsterdam (below left), little John King (below center), and John Julian, a Native American (below right), were among the pirate crew. The map to their left shows the route of the Whydah from her capture to her doom.

Bellamy aboard Whydah
Known capture of ship by Bellamy

miles
0   250   500

NORTH AMERICA

ATLANTIC OCEAN

Cape Cod
April, 26 17 17
Whydah sinks in storm

40° N

35° N

30° N

Gulf of Mexico

Bahamas

West Indies

Cuba

Caribbean Sea

Jamaica

Hispaniola

Tropic of Cancer

February 17 17 Bellamy captures Whydah

20° N

80° W   75° W   70° W

VT
NH
NY
MA
CT
PA
NJ
MD
DE
VA
NC
SC
AL
GA
FL

The Articles

Pirates like Sam Bellamy attacked the ships of all nations. Since they obeyed no country's laws, pirates made up their own. These laws were known as the "Articles", or the "Rules."

As you can see, Bellamy's crew wanted the *Whydah* run democratically, with everyone having an equal say. They wanted the ship to be orderly, but without the hard discipline of merchant or naval service. They wanted their loot to be shared equally. They even wanted to make sure that any injured pirate would be provided for.

This was very different from the way things were run "back home" in Europe.

Even though the pirates were criminals, they insisted that the Articles be strictly obeyed.

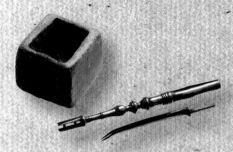

Pirates signed the Articles with pen and ink.

Ye Articles of ye Gentlemen of Fortune

Every Man Sworne by Book & Mirror to be true to these Articles, & to his Ship Mates, is to have a Vote in Matters of Importance. He who is not Sworn, shall not Vote.

Every Man to have Equal Right to ye Provisions or Liquors at any time & to use them at Pleasure, unless Scarcity makes a Restrction necessary for ye Good of All.

Every Man to be called fairly a Board Prizes in turn by the List of ye Company. Every Boarder is to have a Suit of Cloaths from ye Prize.

The Captain & Officers are to be chosen on Commencement of a Voyage, & on any other Occasion as ye Company shall deeme fit.

The Power of ye Captain is Supream in Chace or Battle. He may beat, cut, or shoot any who dares Deny his Command on such Occasions. In all other Matters whatsoever he is to be Governed by the Will of ye Company.

Every Man shall obey Civill Command.

He who first sees a Sail, shall have ye best Pistol, or Small Arm, from a Board her.

Ye Quarter-Master shall be first a Board any Prize. He is to separate for ye Company's Use what he sees fit & shall have Trust of ye Common Stock & Treasurey until it be Shared. He shall Keep a Book shewing each Man's Share, & each Man may draw from ye Common Stock & Treasurey against his Share upon Request.

Any Man who should Defraud ye Company, or another, to ye Vallew of a Dollar, he shall suffer Punishment as ye Company deems fit.

Each Man to keep his Musket, Pistolls, & Cutlass cleane & fit for Service, upon Inspection by ye Quarter-Master.

No Prudent Woman, or Boy, is to be brought a board. No Married Man is to be forced to serve our Company.

Good Quarters to be Granted when Called for.

Any Man who Deserts ye Company, keeps any secret, or Deserts his Station in Time of Battle, shall be punished by Death, Marooning, or Whipping, as ye Company shall deeme fit & Just.

Not a Word shall be Written by any Man unless it be nailed Publickly to ye Mast.

Any Man who Strikes or Abuses another of our Company shall suffer such Punishement as ye Company shall deeme ffit & Just. Every Man's Quarrel to be settled a shoar with Sword & Pistol & be Adjudged Fair Fight by ye Quarter-Master.

All Lights & candles to be put out before 8 a Clock at night. If any Man continues Drinking after that Hour, he must do it on ye open Deck. That Man who shall Smoak tobacko in ye Hold without a Cap on his Pipe, or carry a lit Candle without a Lanthorn, shall suffer Moses Law (40 Stripes less one) on his bare Back.

No Man to talk of breaking up our Way of Living until Each has shared a Thousand Pounds.

If any Man should lose a Limb, or become a Cripple, he is to have 800 Dollars out of ye Common Stock, & for lesser hurts, Proportionably.

Ye Captain & Quarter-Master are to have two Shares of a Prize, the Sailing Master,

Boatswain, Gunner & Surgeon, One Share & a Half. Other Officers One & a Quarter Share. Each Man shall share Plunder Equally. Boys shall have a Half Share.

*In lart part from Captain Charles Johnson's *A General History of the Pyrates*, 1724. Also based on known practices of Bellamy's crew recorded in primary source documents.

Flying the Jolly Roger

Pirates designed their own flags so that they could identify themselves, and also to scare those that they were attacking. Each crew usually had a different flag. Sam Bellamy's was a very large black banner with a skull and crossbones on it. It was called a "Jolly Roger." "Roger" was slang for a footloose rascal in those days.

Flag flown by New England pirate Ned Low

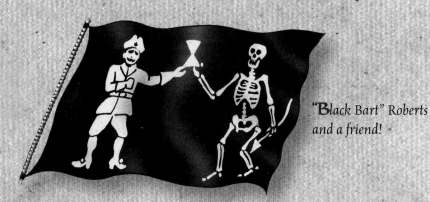

"Black Bart" Roberts and a friend!

Flag thought to be flown by Christopher Condent

ABH AMH

Another flag used by "Black Bart."

High winds and heavy seas drove the Whydah toward shore.

The Storm at Sea

After capturing the *Whydah*, the pirates sailed north, robbing more rich ships on the way. Old Cape Cod stories say that Sam Bellamy was coming back for his girlfriend.

What's for sure is that the *Whydah* and three other ships Bellamy had captured were struck by a storm off Cape Cod on the night of April 26, 1717. The worst New England storm of record, it tore a channel clear across the Cape!

The seas around the Cape are known as "the Graveyard of the Atlantic" because they are so dangerous. Wind gusts perhaps over 80 miles per hour drove the *Whydah* onto a sandbar just 500 feet from shore. Slammed by waves up to twenty feet high, the mainmast soon snapped. The *Whydah* was pushed off the sandbar and capsized.

She was carrying about forty extra cannon and tons of lead in her hold and, when she turned over, all these came crashing down through the decks, shattering her hull and pinning men to the seafloor.

There were 145 men—and at least one boy—aboard the *Whydah*. Only two made it ashore alive. The rest died in the dark, cold water.

Sam Bellamy was just 29 years old, and his crew had taken over fifty ships in a year's time.

The *Whydah*'s riches quickly sank to the bottom and were swallowed up by the shifting sands of the Cape.

And there they stayed for nearly three hundred years...

Deadeyes were used to secure ships' rigging, or ropes.

Traces of the *Whydah*

Objects from the *Whydah* have been in the ocean so long that they are completely soaked with seawater. Eroded metal, rocks, and sand build up on them, and many are shapeless encrusted lumps.

As soon as we bring something to the surface, we start work to conserve it. Sometimes it takes years to preserve a shoe, or a tea kettle, but it's worth the work.

Think of a shipwreck as being a time capsule from the period when it sank. Each object from the time capsule of the *Whydah* tells us a story about what life aboard her was like.

The base of this kettle fit into the ship's stove so that it wouldn't tip over in high seas.

At night, candles in lanterns or pewter candle-sticks were the only source of light. Ships caught fire easily, and so these were used sparingly.

Fork, plate, and spoon. Many of these have markings, such as initials or special symbols, which tell us about those who ate with them.

Pinned to the seabed by a falling cannon, this shoe, leg bone, and French silk stocking are all that remain of John King, youngest of the Whydah pirates.

Pirates liked fine clothes and would steal them from their victims. These cufflinks and silver buttons were high fashion in 1717.

Brass scales were used to carefully measure such valuable materials as medicine or rare African gold jewelry.

Navigational dividers were made in different sizes to suit their owners. They were used to measure distances and plot positions to accurately chart a course.

This pure gold ring from a pirate's hoard was made for a small finger. We have tried to decode the mysterious hand-carved letters, but no luck so far.

Pirates Prized their Weapons

Although the real pirates of history did not fight nearly as often as pirates in the movies, we've found that they still took great time and trouble to make sure that they had plenty of weapons—and the right kind of weapons—to commit their robberies.

Pirates did not want to sink ships, and so they relied on muskets, pistols, and swords when attacking other vessels. They also made a big show of acting as fierce as possible. The best weapon from a captured ship went to the first man to board her.

This is an especially fine flintlock pistol. A pair of these would have been carried on the silk ribbon and slung around a pirate's neck.

Pirates kept lead shot and gunpowder in leather pouches attached to their belts.

Cannon were used against naval vessels, and heavily-armed merchant ships that chose to fight rather than surrender.

While large iron round-shot like this could punch through a ship's hull, most of the Whydah's cannon were loaded with smaller musket balls so they would do less damage.

The barrel and the stock of this musket were cut down by its pirate owner to make it easier to use in close combat

Steel breaks down in salt-water and only the brass hilts of these pirate swords have survived.

Pirates fired bar shot from cannon in order to tear up the sails of ships they were chasing. Bar shot spun like a buzz saw when it hit a target!

The *Whydah* Pirates Meet Their Fate

Other ships under Bellamy's command were damaged in the storm of April 26, and a total of nine pirates were captured.

The two that survived from the *Whydah* were the Native American John Julian, and a carpenter named Thomas Davis. The others were Hendrick Quintor, John Brown of Jamaica, Thomas South from England, Jean Shuan of France, a Swede named Peter Cornelius Hoof, Thomas Baker, and Simon van Vorst of New York. They were imprisoned in Boston for over five months before being put on trial.

Piracy was considered especially wicked, and so the men were tried under special Admiralty Court proceedings. Instead of a jury, their guilt or innocence would be decided by specially-appointed judges.

Thomas Davis and Thomas South convinced the court that they had been forced to join the pirates.

Julian never stood trial. We believe he was sold into slavery. The others were found guilty and, on November 15, 1717, they were brought to the gallows.

After being hanged until they were dead, their bodies were buried on the beach between the high tide and low tide marks because their crimes were committed at sea.

Executed pirates were hung in iron frames called "gibbets" as an example.

Bellamy's men on trial in Boston for piracy

300 Years Later

I first began searching for the *Whydah* in libraries, looking for clues in old records. An old chart from 1717 helped a lot. When I felt sure I knew where the *Whydah* was, I put together a boat, a crew, and all the gear we'd need.

I knew finding the *Whydah* wouldn't be easy. The wreck is close to shore, and, for most of the year, strong winds kick up surf, making it impossible to dive and search.

The wreck would be covered with sand, so we began by using electronic sensing gear that marked the presence of metal. To blow away the sand covering these targets, we fit a special plate on to the boat to direct the wake of the propeller downward.

We searched for over a year and half. By July 1984, we were almost ready to give up, when a diver came to the surface and said there were cannon in the bottom of the thirty-foot pit we had dug! And I will never forget the coin we brought up on the very next dive...

It took another year to prove we had found the *Whydah*. Cape Cod is dangerous, and there've been many shipwrecks off its shores.

After years of research, it was time to dive!

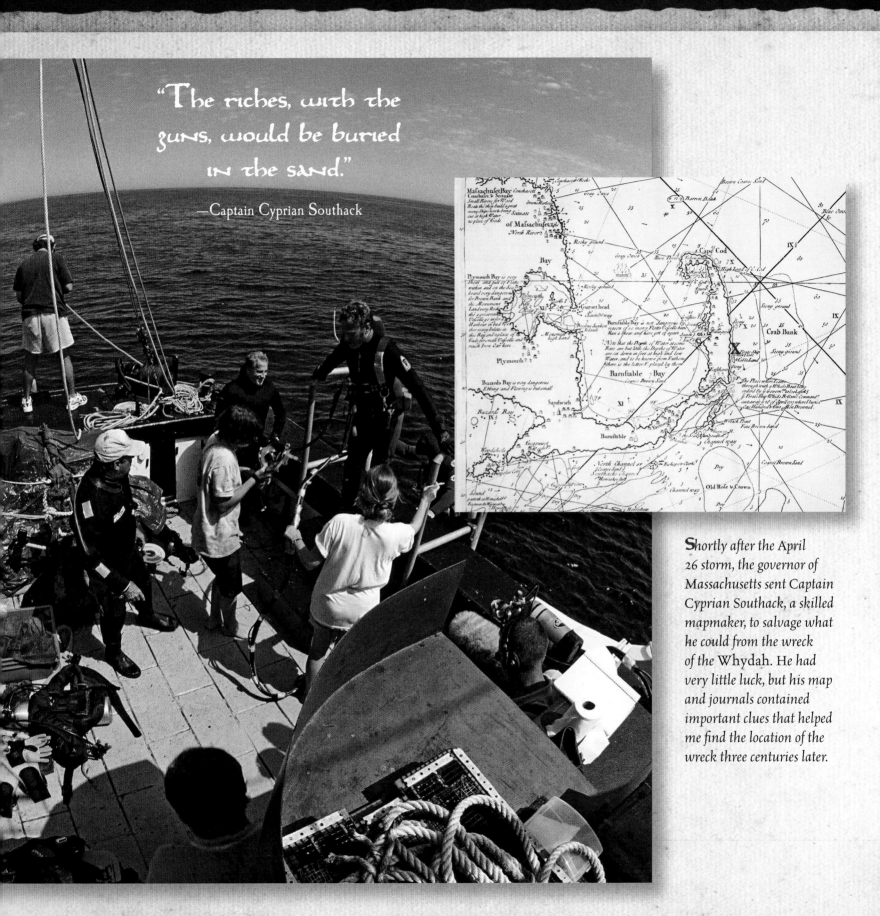

"The riches, with the guns, would be buried in the sand."

—Captain Cyprian Southack

Shortly after the April 26 storm, the governor of Massachusetts sent Captain Cyprian Southack, a skilled mapmaker, to salvage what he could from the wreck of the Whydah. He had very little luck, but his map and journals contained important clues that helped me find the location of the wreck three centuries later.

Pirate Treasure!

Treasure was one of the dreams that led me to search for the *Whydah*. It was one of the best moments in my life when we found our first cannon and our first Spanish silver coin.

Since Spain controlled most of the silver and gold mines in America, a large number of the coins robbed by pirates were Spanish. The coins came in all shapes and sizes, so they were valued according to their weight.

We do not sell the coins or other artifacts we find. Each object can tell us a little about what life was like centuries ago. Preserving the *Whydah's* history is more important than selling her treasures.

Our divers find coins in the sandy ocean bottom using metal detectors and sharp eyes. We must work quickly, but carefully, because the sand is always moving.

The silver coin shown here is a Spanish "piece of eight." Known as a "Royal Strike," it was minted as a special gift. The hole was probably drilled by a pirate so he could wear it on a necklace as jewelry. Below it are two sides of a gold "doubloon." Even though the two coins weigh the same, gold was 15 times more valuable.

The Bell is the Proof

Identifying an old shipwreck is not easy. That's why the bell, which reads "The *Whydah* Gally 1716" is one of our most valuable recoveries. It proves beyond a doubt that the wreck we found is the *Whydah*.

The bell was the heart and soul of the ship. Life revolved around it. It told the men when to work and when to rest; when to eat and when to sleep. It called them to battle stations in times of danger.

Aboard merchant and naval ships, a bell called the crew to hear the captain's orders. Aboard pirate ships, it called the pirates to common councils where they could have a say in their own future...

And a final clang of the bell may have been the last thing Sam Bellamy and his crew heard as the *Whydah* capsized and broke apart.

The bell itself is made of bronze, and the crosspiece is wood. Even part of the bell rope has survived.

The Work Goes On

Artifacts, such as these cannon, must be kept wet until they can be prepared for display.

Underwater archaeology is not just a matter of finding a shipwreck and bringing up her treasures.

In fact, that's just the beginning of our job. All of the recovered objects have to go through scientific cleaning, preservation, and study. Throughout the process, we need to keep careful records on all of the thousands of things we've found. Many of them are drawn and photographed.

Then we work to include our new discoveries in public exhibits, as well as to describe them in books and news articles. As a former teacher, it's important to me that the secret world of the pirates that we're uncovering be shared with others. We are still finding many of the *Whydah's* treasures. There is enough work left for the rest of my lifetime. And that excites me most of all!

Many objects, such as this tea kettle (above), are still very delicate even after having gone through many months of scientific treatment.

This forklift (left) raises an anchor from its storage tank so our technicians can carefully clean it. Electro-chemical treatments then remove the salt that's soaked into it.

Exhibition Credits

Project Whydah

Barry and Margot Clifford

Brandon Clifford

Lt. Cmdr. Alejandro Barrios

Dr. James Bradley

John de Bry

Robert Cembrola

Sean Graham

Bernie Heinze

Scott Herber

Kenneth J. Kinkor

Bob Lazier

Glen MacDonald

Derek McDonald

Todd Murphy

James Nelson

Jeff and Wesley Spiegel

Allan Tufankjian

Andris Zobs

Arts and Exhibitions International

John Norman, President and Executive Producer

Mark Lach, Senior VP and Artistic Director

Michael Sampliner, COO

Brian Harris, VP, Communications and Marketing

Christina Wright, Project Manager

Richard Bright, Production Manager

Chris Jacobs, Marketing

Jason Simmons, General Manager

National Geographic Society

Terry Garcia, Executive Vice President
Mission Programs

Betty Hudson, Executive Vice President
Communications

Sarah Laskin, Vice President
Mission Programs

Mimi Koumanelis,
Director of Communications

Kathryn Keane,
Director Traveling Exhibitions Development

Fred Hiebert,
Archaeology Fellow

Ford Cochran,
Mission Programs Online

Susan Norton,
Director,
NG Museum

Cincinnati Museum Center

Doug McDonald, Director

Dr. John Fleming,
Vice President for Museums

Exhibition Content, Design, and Installation

Sharon Simpson,
Exhibition Writer
SJS Projects

Tom Fricker,
Exhibition Designer,
Fricker Studio

David Dailing,
Artifact Supervisor

Gregory Manchess, Illustrator

Margaret B. Stogner,
Media Production
Blue Bear Films

Kenneth L. Garrett,
Photography
David Mauk, Music
Composition

Rick Belzer,
Lighting Designer

Sam Rembert, Lighting

Ellen Przybyla
Alan Sprecher
Kenny Warren

Artifact Installation

Lexington Studios,
Exhibition Production,
Richard and Frank Bencivengo
Howard Smith
Richard Bizzy
Jerry Parra
John Hogg

Hunt Design Associates,
Graphic Design,
Heather Watson

Crush Creative,
Graphic Production,
John Gibson

Edwards Technologies,
Audio and Video
Brian Edwards, John Brandt

Joe Powell,
Case Production,
Benosh Productions

Canon Medical Systems,
Canon U.S.A., Inc.
Whit Fowler and Greg Dice

GE Aviation QT NDE Services,
Matt Prefontaine, Graphics
Alan Parente, Graphics

Advisory Panel

Dr. Thomas C. Battle, Director,
Moorland-Spingarn Research Center,
Howard University

Dr. Ira Berlin, Distinguished
University Professor
Department of History
University of Maryland

Dr. W. Jeffrey Bolster,
Professor, Early American,
Caribbean History
University of New Hampshire

Mr. Michael Cottman,
Senior Correspondent
Reach Media, Inc.
President, Black Scuba Divers
Association

Dr. Laurent Dubois,
Associate Professor of History
Michigan State University

Dr. Wendy Wilson Fall,
Associate Professor
Department of Pan African Studies,
Kent State University

Dr. John Fleming,
Vice President for Museums
Cincinnati Museum Center

Dr. Robert L. Harris, Jr.,
Vice-Provost
Cornell University

Dr. Marcus Rediker,
Professor of History
University of Pittsburgh

Dr. Faith Ruffins,
Curator, Division of Home
and Community Life
Smithsonian Institution

Dr. Michael Washington, Chair
African Studies Department
Northern Kentucky University

Dr. Francille Rusan Wilson,
Chair, African American
Studies Department
University of Maryland

Real
Pirates

The Untold Story of
The *Whydah* From
Slave Ship to Pirate Ship

A National Geographic
Exhibition

References and Reading

Barry Clifford with Paul Perry, *Expedition Whydah: The Story of the World's First Excavation of a Pirate Treasure Ship and the Man Who Found Her.* New York: HarperCollins, 1999.

DK Publishing, *Shipwreck.* New York: DK Eyewitness Books, 2005.

J. Patrick Lewis, *Blackbeard: The Pirate King.* Washington, D. C.: National Geographic, 2006.

John Malam, *How to be a Pirate.* Washington, D. C.: National Geographic, 2005.

Richard Platt, *Pirate.* New York: DK Eyewitness Books, 2007.

Web Sites of Interest

Expedition Whydah.
Whydah Museum, Provincetown, Mass.
http://www.whydah.com

Real Pirates: The Untold Story of The Whydah from slave ship to pirate ship.
National Geographic Society, Washington, D.C.
http://www.nationalgeographic.com/mission/real-pirates

Pirate Ship Whydah.
National Geographic Society, Washington, D.C.
http://www.nationalgeographic.com/explorer/whydah/index.html

Pirates of the Whydah.
National Geographic Society, Washington, D.C.
http://www.nationalgeographic.com/whydah/story.html

Illustration Credits

Illustrated by Gregory Manchess.

All photographs by Kenneth Garrett unless otherwise noted below:

4 top, Bill Curtsinger / NG Image Collection; 9 right, Roger-Viollet / The Image Works; 12 left, NG Image Collection; 14 right, Shutterstock; 15 all, NG Image Collection; 20 bottom left, Bill Curtsinger / NG Image Collection; 22 left, Topham / The Image Works; 24-25, Brian J. Skerry / NG Image Collection; 26 bottom left, Brian J. Skerry / NG Image Collection; 26 top, Bill Curtsinger / NG Image Collection; 29, Shutterstock; 30 top left, Matthew Prefontaine; 31 top, courtesy Barry Clifford; 31 bottom, Richard T. Nowitz.

It took Eloie Morin 2,138 hours to build this carefully detailed model of the Whydah.

Index

Brandon Clifford, the author's son, has grown up on the Whydah project…

Library of Congress Cataloging-in-Publication
Data available upon request.

Hardcover ISBN: 978-1-4263-0279-4
Library ISBN: 978-1-4263-0280-0

Printed in the United States

Published by the National Geographic Society

John M. Fahey, Jr.,
President and Chief Executive Officer

Gilbert M. Grosvenor,
Chairman of the Board

Nina D. Hoffman, Executive Vice President;
President, Book Publishing Group

Prepared by the Book Division

Nancy Laties Feresten, Vice President,
Editor in Chief, Children's Books

Bea Jackson, Director of Design and
Illustrations, Children's Books

Carl Mehler, Director of Maps

Staff for this Book

Virginia Ann Koeth, Editor

David M. Seager, Art Director

Lori Epstein, Illustrations Editor

Jennifer A. Thornton, Managing Editor

Gary Colbert, Production Director

Lewis Bassford, Production Manager

Susan Borke, Legal and Business Affairs

Manufacturing and Quality Management

Maryclare Tracy, Manager

Nicole Elliott, Manager

Founded in 1888, the National
Geographic Society is one of the larg-
est nonprofit scientific and educational
organizations in the world. It reaches more
than 285 million people worldwide each
month through its official journal, NATIONAL
GEOGRAPHIC, and its four other maga-
zines; the National Geographic Channel;
television documentaries; radio programs;
films; books; videos and DVDs; maps; and
interactive media. National Geographic has
funded more than 8,000 scientific research
projects and supports an education program
combating geographic illiteracy.

For more information, please call
1-800-NGS LINE (647-5463)
or write to the following address:

National Geographic Society
1145 17th Street N.W., Washington, D.C.
20036-4688 U.S.A.

Visit us online at
www.nationalgeographic.com/books

For information about special discounts
for bulk purchases, please contact
National Geographic Books Special Sales:
ngspecsales@ngs.org

For rights or permissions inquiries, please
contact National Geographic Books
Subsidiary Rights: ngbookrights@ngs.org.